Reflections

from

Inner Space

By

Gregory A Geare

ISBN 978-0-578-65229-0
Printed in US
by
Gregory A Geare
P.O.Box 2397
Nevada City, CA 95959
innergreg@gmail.com

For Jessica

CONTENTS

Inner Pleas

Just Wondering

Against the Tide

Inner Pleas

Let It Out

There is this event occurring
It started a while ago
In each of us there is a movement,
A stirring, an awakening
We must let it out, let the spirit out,
Let the thoughts out, let the music out
Push to do something meaningful
Something authentic
Something from below and above us
When you wake up in the morning
Experience the energy, the life,
There's something special happening

Now we talk to each other
We begin to notice it, encourage it
We crave this meaning, this authenticity
We live for this, yet so few others do

There are of course the foreigners
The ordinary people in the world

The ones who are dead and lifeless
They don't know this excitement
This energy-from-elsewhere within us
Emanating in the present-here and now

This is the reality that makes it work
Makes it worthwhile…. makes it fun
Sadly most people don't get it
They aren't aware enough
This is why its's all so lonely
This energy has us, not us it
We don't have it, we are from it
It comes within each of us
It comes with an intention, a purpose

We are not ever alone in our bliss
For we can experience the force in others
Even if they don't recognize it
And do not experience it consciously for themselves
Not being able to share this is a true sadness
I am singing the blues because of them
yet am blissful nonetheless

You Are It

You are the real world
It's the one that you have within yourself
But there is a co-creation at work
With nature and with others
From foreign worlds
Within and without
Not only from you but with you

You are it…. as it is said of old
And the others are also you
Just little ole you
You actually create it all
In conjunction with the
Mysterious and intelligible objects
The natural cosmos
From which we are born

Some of us become lost in the imagined world
Neglecting to understand it critically
Not differentiating fiction from fact

So social confusion abounds
Ironies upon ironies occur
Unseen, unknown by the ordinary mind

When the inner world becomes conscious
And understood objectively
When together with the outer world
We grasp the others in an intentional way
One's view becomes more broad, more real

The known world ever moves
Into the unknown realm
Receding into an ever greater unknown
We can move there in fear or with curiosity
Be repelled or gain wisdom

Be Here With Me

I want to be grounded in the infinite
…...to be up in the land floating above
………..to leave where I am down here
I need a piece of land
Up there
I want to walk on the street above
I want to look below
And be thankful
   For how far I have climbed
       from the lowly valley
To observe it from the peak beyond

Our legacy
Is to give others something
Of our essential self
To share the moment
Saying how it is ….being true and honest

Try not to hide the personal truths
That we are lonely ….and sad

We refuse to reach out and touch
We look down and are sorry
I'm not going there with you yet
No, I won't be the one
      to open up right now
As I turn away from your eyes
The feelings received from you
Are rejected leaving me wrong toward you
      I don't know why
        I can't figure it

I spontaneously defeat my own desire
yet my conscious intention
is only want to be with you
Still I always turn away again and again

We just have a moment
Our present moment is short
      Yet intense
      A lightening strike
      To the earth on which we liv

Child of the spirit

Rise up…. above the ordinary
You'll never know when
They'll come to get you

You tried to have the virgin spirit
But became weary
Of the relentless desires of youth
What you now create
And put forth won't go very far
If you take the usual road
move ahead to a new path

Being alone is …. a nightmare
          but its finding your transformation
Being alone
          is facing the gallows
There is a chance now… to get away
          the noose was tied too loose
Decide….. act now ……..escape
          while the noose is still loose enough

Will their abuse ever end?
Is everything ultimately meaningless?
Know this
It was never our fault,
It wasn't just you
But the whole culture that relativized reality

Now it's us that must bring a new light
Enough light is needed for unexpected friends
We must become truly free together
while there's still a chance

Child of the spirit
Rise up alone in strength
Rise up together with others

You'll never know when
They'll come to get you

Catch Me

I'm falling tonight
Will you catch me??
I'm finally becoming the reality
That was meant for me to be
I'm finally arriving
Where I have always wanted to live

Being in the embrace of one-who-loves-me
Is where I can finally find my true worth
Only here…. do I know humility and trust
        can I aid the cause of truth…
        can I support the voice of me-the-knower
She speaks of her love to a man
This makes it come alive in him
He can't help but react to her beauty and desire
But now he is conscious of how he feels
His love becomes far more intentional..
Than ever before … here…. right now
The man who wants to truly respect
And honor a woman, has a problem for he must

Abnegate himself and be only a vessel for her
We must become "disinterested" ...but can't fully

It's an undeniable fact that a man's animal-self
"lusts" for the body of a beautiful woman
Without conscious intention
He just becomes out of control
And turned on with passion

So how does he honor and promote
Her insight and reflection in such a state?
Impossible!!   Feelings are too strong…..
No choice here
Yet this is how it must be
Nature cannot to be denied

So say yes to the Eros-within
To the purpose of life
To cure what suffering we can
Say yes to the-new life among us
And yes to the heartaches that awaits us

We Human Beings

We human-beings prize our uniqueness
Yet many events occur that are common to us all
So much love that comes, goes
And then comes again
We fall in love
And then just fall

We human-beings
We realize greatness only in humility
Only within inferiority
Can we grasp the profound

The Great Spirit only visits occasionally
Be vigilant, take advantage of such a moment
Only alone can you truly meet such another
Only in sadness can you feel their pain

Welcome the invisible spirits
Ever-possible yet only occasionally present
Oh!! Bring it on you beings-from-the-Beyond

You non-human slackers in eternal bliss
Who know not the dread of death
Only from an inner-voice does this meaning come
Only in this voice can the unknown depths arise

We can speak and understand one another
Offer the human insight which unites strangers

Touch my mind, I so want to hear yours
Being who I want to believe you are....
Or being nothing special like me
Feeling uneasily ...with loneliness
Regret possess me ....as does an anger deep set
within my history............

I am willfully helpless
And diminish my ego strength
for I believe it is not I that feels so powerful
But the great-spirit who comes to visit me...

Only now do I have any hope of being whole
Only with your help can I be who I fully am

I seek an insight into mysteries hidden
For thousands of years
Women often have known them while men have not
Perhaps because they are an "us" when with-child
While a man stands alone always

We all yearn to be a great human being
But we fall short and it's no surprise
We try anyway
We fail and just try again

It's hard being knowingly undeveloped
While sincerely aspiring to be more
It admirable to try transcending one's horizons
Those who have come before us
Exhort us to " keep at it!"
To preserve what has been achieved in the past
We must endure what all humans have had to suffer

Only you can discover that you are one of us
Then you will know that we are all essentially the
same

Sailing Through Mysteries

I awaken to the fact that I am a homeless being
Sailing through a universe
In a galaxy that goes we know not where
Is it even possible for one to ever know?
Or even conceive of such a destination
[At this juncture in time I think not]

I suffered the death of my god with Spinoza
And now I awaken to an aimless path
I accept this in utter solitude without divinity
As no companion could provide a true anchor

My being is necessarily grounded in change
Any friend….. could only be so for a moment
And not possibly accompany me to the very end

How then can I decide what's best in any moment?
To what may I aspire?
How could what's next ever truly improve on
what's now?

From what viewpoint can I find my bearings?

A story is then required
A tale to tell of a life
Not devoid of meaning but rich
Still an absurd life…. lived yet forgotten
Ending in unavoidable death

There is the life that we live
And the life of the mind
Our personal historicity
That is lived in the here and now
Then….

In the aspirations of your spirit
Lies a motive for life
In your self-correcting process of knowing
Lies the truth that grounds your being
Now and perhaps beyond now, who knows?
Events like these considerations
Should be recited and remembered
By those who follow

The In-itself

Being alone
A terrifying truth
A fact that could remove the joy
The contact with another brings

Is it certain … I will die alone?
A possibility which challenges all human meaning
If so there would be nothing
that could be built
      that could ever last

Are we alone?
Perhaps… because there has been no one
who could listen and try to understand
The "see-now-be-seen" was a foolish hope
all connection was already lost
As the thou became unconscious
and again is lost-now

Being alone again

Just allowing the words to arise

Accepting what is without will or commitment

Waiting for whatever is given without judgement

(from whom ever is here within me)

Being in the inner realm

Listening to what pushes into me from below

And settling for whatever I get

Moving into the depths

Slipping into unconscious thought and feeling

I sleep and then

Awake and am again here

to greet the new day

and respond to the task that is given

Just Wondering

Wandering

Not lost yet not doing the right thing
Desiring my routine but waiting for the rest
Needing to discover the 'true desire'
The final aspiration, the road to fulfillment
When will be the climax of this interior upheaval
This eruption of the spirit?

Wandering
Not really believing any one special will come by
Just an ordinary life for me
Appreciating the masters of the inner-life
Understanding the literature of the subjective self
Being authentic yet wandering alone

Wandering
Always desiring more, always more
Yet focusing on nothing in particular
Beginning to express it in words
And just leaving it incomplete
The last phase of life is upon me

I desperately feel a task must be set
Do I fear making the wrong choices (I think not)
Or do I fear not desiring enough or at all

Wandering
So that I can avoid myself
and what my life has become
I have all along expected
that the end could be the best
When all the work is done at last
But the work does not end and this best could
become the worse
I have my wisdom, this peaceful knowing
arising in my soul
The wisdom of the here-now-present has thankfully
been with me a long time
So fortunate am I

Wandering

Because I conceive my life today

as a task to be accomplished

A job I refuse to even begin

Meanwhile I continually shame myself

(as I was trained to do)

Concluding that the Dionysian spirit is simply evil

Regretting my animal desire, my choice to relieve

the boring suffering

I know that I have secretly done wrong

I know that I have not been who I should have been

I know that I habitually continue to embrace the

American cultural self that I despise

Wandering

Is waiting.....................

Contacting Nothing

Peel away the layers of reality
Leave the outer world of nature
Abandon the complicated intrusive world of men
Withdraw from the extroverted world entirely
Move into your personal space
Find your beating heart

Go into the inner realm
Close your eyes and focus on the darkness
Be aware of your invisible breath moving out and in
Focus on breathing, forget your preoccupied self
Allow sensations, thoughts and feelings
To arise freely
Try to purposively intend
All that occurs in your consciousness
Be the experience
That directs your attending
To what is

Now wonder

From whence comes this focused attending?

This intending that makes meaning possible

We just are, we wake up in the morning

And what is is there

The being we are just exists

Regardless of the experiences we have

Your being is just there

But where?

What is... exists in an emptiness

It's a being which is from nothing

A being that is encased an absence

Know that the nothing is necessary

Now understand this framework of existence

Nothing was before we were born

And nothing awaits us in our death

Nothing is required for anything to be

There is no need to stop thinking

For the nothing remains even after

we sense or think or feel

Mindfulness is dwelling in one's attentiveness

Intentions dwell in nothingness

for they arise from no-where conscious

Who are you?

The one who breathes, senses, thinks, feels?

Who is it that lurks in the shadows?

No one real yet no one at all?

Allowing What Is

Relaxed at last
Yet the exigence arises
Exciting my being

A pure desire, an élan vital
Beyond the Eros of the human-animal

An intentional spirit
Aspiring to reach the next height
  A new understanding
    A careful self-realization

One must come to desire the here-now moment
No longer caring whether anything is accomplished
Grateful for the time given
To exist and create

Embrace what-is with a disinterested mood
Withdraw egoistic concerns
And at once become even more immersed

Being-here-right-now together with others

Touching another is bliss

A blessed caress without fear or shame

Being-for-another brings a true fulfillment

The personal moment expands

Being present

    Being heard

        Being a sharing

            Being a love

My inquiring mind

Wonders about possible developments

A human-being ever seeks more meaning

Reaching for ever greater heights and broader views

That extend right to the edge of the horizon of the

unknown

This moving-forward

necessitates a new transformation

A conversion into someone-new

A freedom to allow all the feelings

To flow without fear
Outward to contact another
Sustained with a detached disinterest
The paradox is that to care more
One needs to "care-less"
To care freely is to desire nothing for yourself

One need let go of the desiring and fearful self
The ego that inhibits spontaneous expressions
Release the grip of the animal-human self
That is continually so sensitive and hurt

Existence is enough
Being present to another
Is the fulfillment of being-oneself
Understanding will bring us close
Reflection will bring clarity
Willingness enables
The personal dimension to emerge

Being So High

Being so utterly alone
Is this the price of individuation?

Being in the universal-now
The powerful present moment
There can be harmony right now
But only with a 'grin and bear it'

An experience of just being here with you
Here I am for you
Say for me, "I want you "
Say, "I understand"

Can it be that I've caught your interest
Have you've sensed a deep mysterious
Thread within me
You've come a little farther than most
Now we can be here if just for a moment

The higher one gets…

The more one's perspective is expanded

The better an insight is clarified

When you realize that

The universe of galaxies needs you

To have a meaningful existence

Then everything becomes ok

The need for an ultimate purpose

is finally met once and for all.

Let this be so

Find it again and again

Let her come in when she wants to……

It's a no-desire moment for you

So don't even try

Remove attention

Prescind from the experience

Then you're alright

Just the way you are right-now

Don't worry
It's so safe that little trust is required
Don't give it a thought

let it be alright
  [even if you can't]
let something in
  [even if you don't want to]
let it matter for just a moment
  [even if I can't afford to]

Alone With You

one can be imprisoned
in a tower of their own making
a room with no stair for others to find
an unhappiness is hidden within
I dare not seek it or attend to it
Still…. there is the desire
                        to be honest
                                to be true
one could fear condemnation
but this is pure vanity.
to worry about being disliked
is to only consider within
the implicit sources the unhappy emotions
that haunt us.

I keep telling myself
to keep seeking
stop expecting
surrender
to this moment

yet I find only what I imagine
only what I expected all along

alas…. still trapped
still desiring to reach out
and to grasp someone really there
clearly I identify too much
with my mere creation
blocking the experience of another
alas…. still trapped

My sole purpose
is to overcome this deliberate self-hiding
and for you to somehow recognize
in this expression
the objectification of your own experience of me
It is simply to share…to communicate
to perhaps find a little of me in your image
and to be creative together
come with me to a new land of meaning
words will lead us along
to the new realms we make only for ourselves….

Real Connection

A time of truth
A time of awakening
A time to connect with what's real
Being mindful of *what is* for you right now

Be in the here and now
     In the here and now be meaningful
          The here and now is always

Be in the here
Just now for me
The eternal present
     Being without time yet within it
       Just eternally being who you are

For a moment
I wonder about what it is we are for
What's desired so passionately…..
What I know I could never have
What I want and yet should not

For a moment I'll consider who you are
To make such a difference for me
What makes you such
that I cannot live without you?
Failing to live in your absence
and needing to disregard your impact on me

For a moment
I will let loose without you
I'll be truthful and lasting
I'll care for you without saying so

I seek to assert my message
Hear a truth that's needed to be said
Understand what has been kept from you
Hear the ugly truth
Know that your belief has been wrong
That what once was divinely revealed truth
has become a mere fiction
[I'm avoiding your response here
I'd rather not care if you object]

Be careful not to overvalue the world-of-men
Men have tried to become separate from nature
They die needlessly, they fail to realize
That the soul of man is only
Nature in its earthly glory

Opposites occur all at once
Each one includes an other
Yin and yang together are one reality
Separated only for knowledge, for growth, for
purpose
To be oneself....is to be-for-others
The souls of men are connected to others
As many lights combine to make a light

An individual awakens in the morning
And spontaneously becomes aware
This consciousness is individual yet polymorphic
He then joins a collective shared-awareness
That combines people
With emotional attachments
both negative and positive

Some connections are operative pre consciously
Non-intentional commingling of lives and feelings
Being completely unto ourselves only
Is impossible then
For we are all of the earth
As are all living beings

Enjoy each other without desire
want to know your friend
but not lose myself in them
Not only to touch skin
But capture their intentions
And create meaning together

See now and be seen
By all who are in the "know"
With this in-group there is no fear
No wanting for anything more
No anticipation of what's in it for me
No expectation that you'll do what I expect
The work is done, so relax

Weary of this solitary impulse to do nothing

The pleasures of new development are sought

We become easily confused....

For the aim is so radically new

Indecisive... for there a so few to support us

Some moments are more important than others

Sometimes you just have to drop everything

Against the Tide

A Great Suffering

It is great suffering
To have never been loved completely
(or even enough)
Even by one's mother, by one's father
Or the many others along the way
I have tried to love another with great purpose
And have not persevered in any lasting way
I have not endured in any authentic way
I have felt internally what could be true love
Sought the simple love of a woman
Hoping for love without condition, without shame
And yet know it is beyond me......
This is truly great suffering, a great loss
This great experience of human existence
Has been lost to me, yet this must not remain so
My aged despair is tempered
By a fleeting hope for some change
Yet I am confounded
It all this makes so little sense

To have one's essential fate
In the hands of another who never appears

Turning to some higher purpose
Does not arise in me anymore
For it did not satisfy my infinite desire
Love of humanity inspires so many
But this is a distraction I cannot afford
I long to begin intentionally giving myself
To a mysterious presence in my consciousness
This is a joyous sadness, a pleasant contradiction
For there is a great love within me
Shared so rarely and without purpose
An inter-personal love is apparently forbidden me
And I flee into celibacy for a survival
I've just never been able to love another deeply
I'm left with the yearning, the desire, the mystery
I cry at the loss of any true fulfillment
Still, I have some peace, some satisfaction
I cannot comprehend why… this contented feeling
is enough to carry me forward

Alone Without God

I mourn the death of my God
My lord who gave my life purpose and meaning
I cry for I almost found Him
Only to confront just-myself again
I cannot give my life a point
I must find this outside myself
The need to connect with another is essential
Yet I don't, I can't, I mustn't

A torture this suffering
So many have a God to bring them their joy
That is beyond mere human companionship
My fate is to know too much
To know all existence is simply in me
And no other

Yet I am torn within my spirit
I yearn with an infinite fate to really connect
With someone, with anyone, with anything
No mere depression is this

But the state of any human being
We are each defined as a being incomplete
One who strives always to know more
To affirm oneself in the act of grasping-a-fact
Being in a reality in which I am adrift
without a dream
I cannot just create a meaningful goal
For any creation, any dream, any image
Is just me being who I am
One needing the touch of one greater than me

These terrible truths strike me down
I can only know
what is in my senses and imagination
The world is only what I experience it to be
Yet I can transcend myself
in the movement of grasping-a-fact
With certitude, I venture into an other world
Where phantom objects swarm enticingly in
A self-play. A relation-who-relates-himself to self
Only me-here-now

So I turn farther within
Go deep into my dreams
Encounter the kiss of the feminine spirit
Waiting there for us
An encounter with the depth-world
A personal-collective-connection

I am alone
The terrifying truth
The fact that removes the joy
The contact with another brings

I am alone
Is certain for I will die alone
The fact that challenges all human meaning
There is nothing to build that could ever last

I am alone
There is no one who could listen and understand
The hope "see-now-and-be-seen" was foolish
The Thou has been lost

I am alone

Allowing the words to arise

Accepting without will or commitment

Waiting for whatever is given

I am alone

Listening to what pushes into me

Settling for whatever I get

Slipping into unconscious thought and feeling

I sleep and then

I awake alone

I greet the new day

I respond to the task that is given

Where is the value

That will justify a life?

It is easy to reject worldly riches and distractions

It is hard to find something to serve

I am such an egg waiting to be cracked-up

To be a new life or just be a lost soul

A living-dying-existence

A being-human for a moment
Then a be-gone as so many uncountable others

I worry…. for I once had a God
who was present to me
One I took comfort in,
since He justified my whole existence
And taught me the value of my action, my being
To such an extent that I could accept an agape-love
and be Christ-like
And just be connected

There is this life force that flows
This energy that enlivens, is it's source
Me or another?

I am just one existence
For when I end, it's simply over
I drift in an unknown
With futility………. I await the next-now
Again, I will serve the security-habit

hoping for a change

I worry……
Will I be the only one to read the words
Understand the thoughts?
Will it be only a just-me here?.

There is no sadness
In accepting that one's fate
Is identical to that of all human beings

The Greater Self

Allowing the Greater Self to arise
is to become more aware
It's doing a little better than the ordinary
A confidant energy arises
The peace of being carried along
Willingness at rest
We do not surrender our will to this Great Self
But intentionally allow and promote
The feeling that is from beyond when it arises
Periods of consolation come at times
But then we can become desolate as well
We are elated in the numinous moment
And still we cry in despair when left alone
A greater (divine) presence may exist
Whether acknowledged or not
Take comfort in this possibility

This special experience
Is but one of many moments in time
There is sleeping, working, being entertained
There are family moments
And numinous experiences
Each in their own time.

I endure being torn between two realities
One visible and one not so
Fear of the unknown tears me asunder
Even while I remain whole
I yearn to commune with another
I am desperate to share what I have been given
And am mystified at the difficulty in this
My lot seems to be to discover
How to be with another
While remaining completely alone

Chaos Land

Understanding reality
Has become less relevant to most
Yet wonder abounds nonetheless

Right now is the new
"come off it" and "be-here-now"

Right now we are alive
Bounded only by the limits of our imagination
All is relative to our perspective

There is no secure ground beneath us
There's no floor under the universe,
We are not any where except on the move
Knowing this is unsettling to be sure
The only real time is right-now

No worries…..
for new surprises
Are always waiting at the door

The wonders become present
What is new for me could be enough for now
And then I skillfully survive
I am new-in-the-now
I create my land again

No worry…..
for new surprises
Are always waiting at the door

Welcome to chaos-land
All reality and value are determined
By each individual
who cares to do so in his own way
While so many others are swept along

I want this to mean-something-to-you
I want the hidden excitement be-for-us-now

So reach out and say "I'm scared to see you"
Afraid to touch you, yet hoping to know you

An impossible turn of events occurs
The impossible commitment
that I am only here-for-you reveals itself
fulfilling your desires
without cares or anticipations
A plea that you try to read my mind

Welcome to chaos-land
Where reality can only be what you imagine it to be
Still, for us there are "hidden patterns" in the depths
True understandings it be discovered
The here-and-now is continually presenting them

But is this spontaneous emergence of thought and
feeling a threat to the normal course of one's life?

Stability and responsibility are essential but the
natural spontaneous revelations from the depths of
one's soul cannot be denied.

Confessing

When we confess to someone
We give them a power over us
If we let them sincerely know
a portion of our selves
Then they "have us" in that respect
When we open up and share

We know that their peek into our soul might hurt
There is a chance a bit of our essence might be lost
We resist a bondage to she-who-must-be-obeyed
Our efforts can be only for freedom
Losing the delight of submitting to a Lord

The solitude freedom brings can be as a prison
We desperately desire to communicate to others
To somehow express our inner-self to them
But this private-world is too subtle to be spoken
Adequate music is helpful but usually can come
only from their inner-selves of gifted artists.

I have but a little music to offer

And my personal life remains secluded

I am locked in here

No means appears to open a window

And let my soul speak

So I wander.....lost.... there is no other

From which to get a bearing

I am locked into the fact that for me

Everyone can only be how I perceive them to be

And so I fail to encounter them in a real way

Let Go

Let go
Let the spirit arise
Don't be afraid
Be humble now
Your ego is falling
And could shatter
Who you know yourself to be
Is near its end

Yet being humanly present might remain
After death nonetheless
Despair is an absence of a supposed divine spirit
A misfortune grounded in emotional belief
For to not doubt God is absurd
As He is not actually out there
But only a creation of our imagination

Knowledge of a divine spirit is simply impossible as
Anything we know has to be first experienced
within our human consciousness.

There is an intelligence in all matter
As it continually organizes itself in patterns
And then becomes a self-correcting process
That enables an evolution of the integration of
energy and matter into human life
This fact moves you further along to a real truth

Look out for the subtle interference
Of the endangered ego here
It rules your presence before others
And is the source of your hopeless yearning

Allow greatness to arise
Yet lay no claim to the result
As the greater self is responsible
We are but inadequate expressions
We are a mere great wave
Of the immense ocean we make real

Meeting Inside

So I'm afraid to speak freely
If I say what I know
I'm afraid you'll just put me off
And we'll lose the precious contact

I am easily spontaneous-with-others each day
A paradox when considered thoughtfully
I want to be more intelligent
I even want to be bigger than life
I want to live in the timeless-now
I want to be free to say what comes to mind
I want to be proud of who I've become

A negative feeling arises with these egoistic desires
The wrongness of being selfish
(living for one's own pleasures)
So I become afraid to "be-smart", be honest,
be insightful in public
This fear just shuts me down

Be mindful

    Be present

        Be spontaneous

            Be yourself

                Be for others

Let the laughter come back

Embrace the eyes that offer themselves to you

Enjoy them without undue desire

Wonder how meaningful and mysterious they are

Deep anxiety has arisen

You've pried into me

I opened up anxiously and

You laughed away my fears

Where are we headed?

[a dreaded question]

Know this...I let my guard down

Not ever so freely as this

For you have already disarmed me
You demand that I speak the truth
It's my favorite unspeakable thing to do
An honest outburst is needed

I will tell you a secret
(I've only told myself once before)
"What can I confess to myself?"
Could this be my path to real self-control?
I want to speak to you with importance
I want to express my power
[if you could only accept it]
A glow that increases
as the moments with you lingers
I want you to know that I am someone greater
When I speak to you and listen

 A lover would be one who can listen
Without reservation, without distraction
So grasp the essence of another
What is this essence??

[72]

Is it who you are, yet who you could (will) be?

Perhaps, for your friends

May still know essential things about you

Things you are not aware of…

True friends are essential

Without allies we suffer an intolerable solitude

Can you have enough yourself and need no other?

Be strange yet complete?

My love

I want you to experience what I experience

Understand what I know to be real

I've wandered into you

You say "Hey"

I can only quietly withdraw

As I fear being exposed as an ignorant fool

And laughed at for being so odd

[the group scares me so]

If I stop playing the game

I could lose my wealth, my job,

my family, my home

You say "yes" and invite me in
But my *yes* just doesn't last

I'm afraid you'll pick me blind
(because I am for only you and
I've been hurt before)
My heart is broken and shattered

I'm afraid we won't be real
And I'll simply have to return
to my familiar room of dreams
Just killin' time with some fantasy

I am trapped in an inner prison of my own creation
It seems that I can't know
what your really like until I get free
So I can only speak to my fantasy of you...sorry...

Mend My Heart

be with oneself ……..*alone*

try to face it now

accept the fear

experience the dread

let it know you now

let it know you

experience the terror

go to where it will take you

open up to the coming dread

let it have you

be alone now

how could this be better?

it's just you now

let their personal truths be known

      let them have their pain

            let them have their truth

being here
to get the work done
being awake
now suffer the darkness from below

here we are
seeking a new point-of-view
be ready to be different
      and take it from them again
ready to prevail
      and welcome them all in

here we are
going where we must
going away in sorrow
coming to the new truth
coming all the way

we need something to live for
      something to care about
           someone to listen to
                someone who knows us

be with me
just as i am
this can be a time to touch
you are here
tell me….tell us all
what will open our truth within
each moment i am for you

again
tell me what you want
tell me now
tell me so I won't forget
tell me …..you must
because of the sorrow we share

I am lost in grief
I drift off and neglect to say
how we rise above the suffering
and leave the ordinary worlds

tell me

let me feel that you know me

mend my heart ... it breaks so

only with you can I open up

only with you am I truly spontaneous

with you progress is finally made

we can we break out of this doldrum together

tell me now

tell me what you're willing to do.....

        who you're willing to be.........

Shedding the Mask

what mask can a man create
to face his goddess

to relate to such an immense force
is a daunting task

seeing two flames when there is only one
a change in perception
tricking his mind as to which is truly real

a man usually feels a necessity to
pledge his servitude, his suffering to Her
men want to give her their obedience and effort
yet they project this desire for Her
unconsciously on to many feminine souls
who willingly receive this masculine advance

they receive him yet are unable to carry
the weight of Her force thrown upon them

the great feminine spirit
influences men to give more of themselves
to change direction when necessary
even to go down where death dwells
fearing this..... men cry out that they are too weak

she has a force
a strength to be reckoned with
a force known to be a push from or pull upon one

she has an influence that matters
bringing objects that are meaningful and relevant

forces can be visible or invisible to the eye
men must learn that it is not ocular vision that gives
reality
but a factual understanding that makes something
real
men are helpless but to submit to this force
or otherwise chose it
it is merely given
as is life itself

it would be a proper reward
to decide to serve this goddess
who is given such power
but then his choice matters little

yet
to be authentic
he must bear his soul
open his heart to what is given
both unconsciously and consciously

modern man must then divest
himself of his cleverly crafted mask
the persona with which he presents himself to others
yet all the while hiding his true personal self

yes, he is able to sing the blues
but only as well as he is able to detach himself
while taking each day as it comes

so the time has come

for him to be personal with another

to lose the mask

    and craft a language

        to speak his new self-revelation

only by expressing himself

in a personal way with others

can a bond of true love be created

Silent Thought

with trust a relationship is uneventful
without it, the relationship becomes interesting
with love the union is worth it
without it, life becomes conflicted

one doesn't always cause his conflicts alone
one person isn't entirely different from the other
because what he wills
or what she intends alone
this is only real because we grasp it
yet the differences arise without personal effort
the opposition is already there in our natural being

a muse comes and is greeted with joy
and with a wager that challenges us to continue
to produce…. to play… with values
rewards will be reaped
the muse comes only to speak her approval
while another spirit comes to share and inspire

a secret feeling raises you up

a secret which is a private bond with creation

a secret that is for no-one-but-you

a secret only perceived here-and-now

a secret that never entirely ends

it is here for you just this once

a moment that begins

and drifts of into eternity

silence enables receptivity

      silence is giving the other reality permission

      in silence we can accept *what-is*

      we can find our wonder in silence

      listen for a clue

      listen, that's enough!

silence is entering into nothing

quietly walk through the forest

quietly attend to what's important

quietly enable what is felt to be real-in-the-moment

quietly withdraw for *her* sake,

for *their* meanings...... for *his* spirit

www.ingramcontent.com/pod-product-compliance
Lightning Source LLC
Chambersburg PA
CBHW020515030426
42337CB00011B/397